No Peace Doves on the Olive Tree

Poems for Palestine

Nabeela Khan

Table of Contents

Dedication 5

Introduction 7

Author Biography 9

Poems 10

   1. Let's Call A Spade A Spade. 11

   2. No Peace Dove On The Olive Tree. 15

   3. Silence Is The Food That Fuels A Genocide 17

   4. Israel Has Shot The Peace Dove 23

   5. Israel Has Silenced Their Voices 25

   6. Again And Again 31

   7. A Topsy-Turvy World 37

   8. Heroes 45

   9. Take 51

   10. My Name 55

   11. Tatreez 63

   12. Children Of Gaza 67

   13. Racism Rally 71

14. What Did You Do? 77

15. We March.. 79

16. We Watched 81

17. Can You?... 85

18. Don't You Ever Think That We Have Forgotten You... 87

19. I Will. I Wish 89

20. Chant For Our March.. 91

Dedication

I would like to dedicate this book to the resilient souls of Palestine, who's sacrifices echo through the ages.

May these verses honour your strength, preserve your stories, and illuminate the path of hope, for generations to come.

In memory of those who have sacrificed everything, and in solidarity with those who continue to strive for peace.

Jazak'Allah Kheir.
(May God Reward You with Goodness)

100% of funds raised from this book will be donated to aid the People of Palestine.

DEDICATION

Introduction

Thank you for buying this book and supporting the Palestinian people.

I vividly remember watching the news in the 1990s, witnessing the devastation as Israel launched military operations in Gaza. Chillingly referred to as "mowing the lawn."

I was shocked, overwhelmed by a sense of helplessness.

Whenever I tried to speak about it, the response was always the same: "There's nothing we can do."

In that moment, I turned to poetry. I put pen to paper and wrote my first poem.

Just as an attempt to process the horror and give voice to the voiceless. That was nearly 30 years ago. Since then, the situation in Palestine has only deteriorated. The cycle of violence has continued and escalated into a genocide.

As Edmund Burke once said, "The only thing necessary for the triumph of evil is for good men to do nothing."

Today, we choose NOT to do nothing, not to remain silent. We choose not to stand by helpless. We refuse to allow evil to triumph.

INTRODUCTION

I share that first poem now, not only as a reflection of the past but as a witness to the ongoing tragedy. Through words, through poetry, we bear witness. And through collective action, we can make a difference. Not just by remembering, but by boycotting and demanding change. By standing against apartheid. By standing against genocide.

Until Palestine is free.

Author Biography

Nabeela studied Fashion Design and Textiles at Central Saint Martins in London, where she received her bachelor's degree. Later, she pursued her passion for education, completing a Postgraduate Certificate in Education and Training in Bradford.

Deeply committed to justice and a passionate advocate for Palestine, Nabeela channels her creativity and activism into every aspect of her life.

She teaches and remains actively involved in a wide range of community initiatives. Whether its leading cookery classes, sewing, pattern cutting and recycling workshops, craft or charity projects; Nabeela brings energy, imagination, and purpose to everything she does.

Through the pages of this book, Nabeela invites you to witness, to reflect, and above all, to act.

"We know too well that our freedom is incomplete without the freedom of the Palestinians." Nelson Mandela

Poems

Let's call a spade a spade.

Bismillah

Dying children.
Burning homes.
War crimes.
Broken bones.
Innocent children getting shot.
Guilty people saying they're not.
With bombs that drop like acid rain, don't let our voices be in vain.
Why don't we people ever learn.
It's only freedom that they yearn.
It's only freedom that they yearn.
Babies screaming covered in blood.
You know Israel will do no good.
We sit back and think it's far away.
Get on with life, work rest and play.
But it will hit our door steps, it already has done.
Would you sit back if it was your sister or mum?
Would you?
Could you?
There's been a stream of genocide, slow and steady.
To kill for land, Israel is always ready.
And if this land could speak?

LET'S CALL A SPADE A SPADE.

Imagine what it would say.

"So much blood from the innocent I've taken every day.

My olive trees a million and more have been destroyed from their roots.

Thousands of animals killed, who grazed on me, it's not just humans that they shoot.

My paths, roads rivers, run with blood, then my soil takes on the burden,

Then together with time they hide the crime, but not for long I'm certain.

Is this genocide not enough for the world to wake up, and see?

I'm the holy land because of God, no need to shoot guns in me.

And as I see what's happening to my people, I think has the world gone blind?

They just don't care for the human race, or is it because it's Muslim kind?

So, what can we do to stop this killing?

Could we ever teach people compassion?

To see life as life, wherever you live,

Could we make peace the fashion?

You see, the media act like these killings are something new,

But Israel bombing Palestinians is giving me déjà vu.

I've seen it for years and Israel is never condemned.

NO PEACE DOVES ON THE OLIVE TREE

They are the killers but were told to feel sorry for them.

So let's call a spade a spade, it's an apartheid regime.

Openly aggressive, racist, colonial power, crushing every Palestinians dream.

Committing crimes against humanity, they are cruel beyond belief.

Systematically depriving them of human rights,

They don't want any kind of peace.

They practice prolonged segregation and institutionalised racist oppression.

Controlling food, water, fuel, education, it's all at their discretion.

So if you support this Zionist agenda and believe the lies that they say,

Try living a day as a Palestinian and then come tell me that's ok.

People, now is the time to boycott.

Join the PSC,

Join the BDS movement,

It's time Palestine was free.

Don't vote for lying politicians who have blood on their hands.

Make your voices loud and heard so everyone can understand,

LET'S CALL A SPADE A SPADE.

That we won't stand for any more murders of babies and their mothers.

They can dehumanise them all they want , but they'll always be our sisters and brothers,

Our mothers.

Our lovers.

And we stand strong in solidarity, for them and for all humanity.

because one day it will become a reality,

Just you wait and see.

Palestine will be free.

Insha'Allah.

> People, now is the time to boycott.
> Join the PSC
> Join the BDS movement.
> It's time Palestine was free.

No Peace Dove on the olive tree.

Bismillah

No peace dove on the olive tree.
Israel shot it.
Did you see?
Zionists speak about peace? That's just absurd.
They just want to shoot the God damn bird
They'll never hold the olive branch out
They'll take every last tree by force, no doubt.
As U.S. sends Israel Hellfire missiles, the UK, parts of drones and planes.
Their diplomacy licences terrorism.
They are murderers all the same.
Enabling genocide with no shame.
They can't send a bottle of water to Palestine.
What kind of people?, what kind of crime.?
Little Babies bodies grey.
Under rubble, lost they lay.
Starving mothers no milk to feed.
Bury their new borns as they plead
Fathers run, bleeding babes in arms,
He kisses her to keep her calm.
No hospitals to help them heal,
Can you imagine? This shit is real!

NO PEACE DOVE ON THE OLIVE TREE.

Nowhere to go, nowhere to hide.

They can't escape this genocide.

No peace dove on the olive tree.

Israel shot it.

Did you see?

Did you see them?

Did you cry?

Did you condemn Israel?

Did you ask why?

All countries surrounding Palestine will answer for their silent crime.

If not in this world, then in the next they will.

After a genocide, silent still?

Silence is the Food that Fuels a Genocide

Bismillah

There is one thing believe,
I don't think I'm being naïve,
But Gaza is not under occupation by Israel,
It's the rest of the world that is!
Not only occupied,
Complicit in lies,
Accomplices in crime,
Conspiracies divine,
Employed, recruited,
The truth diluted,
All their actions and lies have proved,
Zionism must be removed.
They can't try to justify the unjustifiable,
For the destruction and death, they are liable.
They have created a hell with this genocide.
Ethnic cleansing, nowhere to hide.
This horror surpasses description, definition, explanation,
Extermination by settlers.
This is a holocaust.
Genocidal atrocities at their worst,

SILENCE IS THE FOOD THAT FUELS A GENOCIDE

Catastrophe but the world can't see,
So many child amputees!
Horrifying butchery, from the river to the sea.
This is collective punishment,
This is mass murder,
This is starvation of a nation.
Forced displacement,
Snipers targeting children,
Targeting pregnant women,
Targeted killings,
New thresholds of horror, barbarity unleashed.
Massacres increased.
A new-born takes its first breath, fast.
Only to be it's last.
Their grief is beyond belief.
Fascism is rife.
Its spreading worldwide.
They kill with pride.
This is Ethnocide.
The world has lost its moral compass.
As Zionism spreads like some infectious fungus.
Can you see how these maniacs have woven a web of lies.
Justifying genocide.
Dropping bombs from the skies.
Hundreds of thousands died.

NO PEACE DOVES ON THE OLIVE TREE

Cutting off food supplies.
Shackles around ankles,
Cuffs around wrists.
Tape across mouths.
Torture exists.
Blood. Soaked. Eyes.
Children's wrists cable tired.
Orphaned babies scream and cries.
Toddlers shaking traumatised.
Not a second for goodbyes.
And rape is justified!
As humanity dies,
No media asking why's
Psychological violence,
World leaders silence.
Annihilation, extermination,
Evil war crimes denied.
Please take time to analyse.
Genocidal propaganda underlies.
And the UK government complies.
Human animals, they surmise.
Little children they despise.
Soulless monsters won't compromise.
This is the Devil in disguise!
Barbarity has reached unbelievable levels,
As world leaders support these pure evil devils!

SILENCE IS THE FOOD THAT FUELS A GENOCIDE

But guys,

From the ashes, They. Will. Rise.

They have bombed the watermelon and the seeds have exploded across the world.

They can bury them but don't they know?

Those seeds will grow.

For decades they've murdered for this land.

But don't they know the Palestinians will never go.

Their resistance is incredible,

So, they must know.

Their freedom is inevitable.

"It's Israeli land", is what they tell,

But the only land they'll get,

Is in hell.

Inshallah.

But until then, we must shout out loud for justice,

And do it with pride,

Remember silence is the food that fuels a genocide.

NO PEACE DOVES ON THE OLIVE TREE

SILENCE IS THE FOOD THAT FUELS A GENOCIDE

Israel has Shot the Peace Dove

Bismillah

Israel has shot the peace dove!
Destroyed the symbol of peace, hope and love.
The babies are burning in fire,
Death tolls are getting higher.
Drones fill the skies with a burning wire.
No talk of cease fire.
No talk of cease fire.
He said they'd cease fire,
But he's a bloody liar.
They all lied and we believed them,
Now the truth is clear, we must condemn.
They are starving the babies,
Starving old ladies,
Murdering the surgeons.
The twisted truth is their version.
The words they breathe are fake,
Their teachers are teaching hate.
No one to investigate the billion crimes,
They're selling their souls for dimes.
From beneath the fire, the rubble, the ruins,
2 systems, 2 realities, 2 sides
But only 1 word. Apartheid!

ISRAEL HAS SHOT THE PEACE DOVE

Occupied, brutalised, and betrayed by humanity,
Every soul who's stayed silent is complicit in this calamity.
It's time to make the truth louder than the myth.
Remember its peace and justice we must stand with.
The bullets are theirs but the silence is our shame,
We must shout it and mean it,
Never In Our Name.

Israel has Silenced their Voices

Bismillah

Israel has silenced their voices,
But they have only made us louder.
They have built a 30-foot-high apartheid wall,
But only made us stand tall.
They murder the press,
Drag their names through the mud.
But we still hear their stories because they write them in blood.
They murder the babies who had never even been kissed.
But the test of this loss strengthens their determination to exist.
The Palestinians have an unbelievable, unwavering faith.
Another level of belief.
With no doubts they praise and thank Allah in their deepest darkest grief.
And Zionists continue to murder the medics so the injured have no help to heal,
They show the world their cruel cold-blooded brutality is sickening and unreal,
Now Human Rights Watch,
Doctors Without Borders,

ISRAEL HAS SILENCED THEIR VOICES

Amnesty International, has proof all recorded,

Of crimes against humanity of the evilest degree.

All because the Palestinian people want to be free!

They have systematically bombed hospitals and schools,

Disregarded international law. Broken every rule,

And proved every ruler a fool.

We thought the world would have to help when Palestine would call.

But these Kings, Prime Ministers and Presidents have shown they've got no balls!

They talk the talk, shake their heads and say there's nothing they can do.

But how deadly is their silence and their disregard for what is true.

They can't shed a tear when tear gas bombs fall from the sky.

White phosphorus burns children, as Israel cuts off their medical supply.

And leaders of the world just watch and all their cries ignore.

They may not be sending military help but it's their silence that hurts us more.

Their silence!

Louder than orphan child screaming "why?"

Their silence,

Louder than bombs that fall from the sky.

NO PEACE DOVES ON THE OLIVE TREE

They have forced them to live in poverty while settlers take their beautiful homes.

Changed the names of their towns cities and roads creating Jewish only zones.

Stolen their orange, date and olive trees,

Their hummus, their food and their honey bees.

They have taken their human rights away,

But we see what they do and we know how to pray.

We know how to protest, we know how to boycott, we know how to demonstrate,

And we're not going to stop, we're just going to escalate,

Because we know what we permit, we promote.

So crooked politicians won't get our vote!

Those who don't ask for a ceasefire? How crazy is that?

Turn away while children starve, and just watch their wallets getting fat.

Watch while Israel denied, oppressed, silenced, suppressed,

Tortured, imprisoned, they have stolen and lied, then in self-pity, cried!

"Feel sorry for us, we have to defend".

But you'd no need to defend if your bloody, racist, murdering occupation came to an end.

They've proven they're trigger happy and crazy,

Soldiers or settlers, they're fine killing babies.

ISRAEL HAS SILENCED THEIR VOICES

Children throwing stones who try to resist, they're calling them terrorists.

Then they put these kids for years in prison!

Isn't that terrorism?

And those bastards who allowed babies to suffocate in cots,

Beautiful little girls killed by snipers' gunshots.

Little boys bleeding out who just went out to get water,

A pregnant woman protecting her tummy as she's slaughtered.

We see you Palestine.

We hear you Palestine.

We stand beside you Palestine.

And we promise, one day you'll see justice for their crimes.

Inshallah!

NO PEACE DOVES ON THE OLIVE TREE

ISRAEL HAS SILENCED THEIR VOICES

Again and Again

Bismillah

In the heart of this land that once pulsed with life,
The devastation of annihilation cuts like a knife.
Extermination of a nation in modern times,
As we watch unfold a billion crimes.
Its people struggle to remain standing.
With Israel's land grabs expanding.
While missiles rip it apart from its roots,
From every corner a sniper shoots.
Their homes turn into graves,
Their pain, horror, torture wave, after wave, after wave.
Gaza's face diminished by siege.
So, what the hell is it worth, our freedom of speech?
Our freedom of speech? What does that even mean?
World democracy? It's a political smokescreen.
It's actually obscene.
When those who do speak the truth are imprisoned for years,
For closing death factories for caring, for tears.
What is freedom of speech worth, if you cannot condemn a genocide?

AGAIN AND AGAIN

But we will condemn.
We will ensure these murders have nowhere to hide.
We will fight them worldwide.
For their unashamed barbarity, never witnessed in the world's entire history,
There's no mystery,
They trade humanity for hypocrisy.
This is their democracy.
There is no time now for silence, no time to hold your tongue,
In this world stained in Palestinian blood, Gaza's become a graveyard for our young.
Children who used to dream of life are dreaming now of death,
Dreams buried under the rubble,
Traumatised, petrified,
Not a corner they can hide,
Not a morsel of food to eat,
Their whole existence is in delete,
In the shadows of the rubble where silence weeps,
Young children, like little Hind Rajab, lost in endless sleeps.
With eyes like heavenly stars that shimmer and fade,
Each child's dream a soft whisper, now buried in shade,
Laughter once danced on Gaza's warm summer air,

NO PEACE DOVES ON THE OLIVE TREE

Now cries of sorrow, with a heart's heavy longing prayer.

And it's not just little Hind, there are countless more,

Thousands of futures destroyed by their bloody war.

Each name becomes a soft sigh, each soul a lost song,

In a world full of darkness, where they should never ever belong.

They should have run freely, between olive trees full of light.

Shared secrets and giggles skipping under the moonlight,

But their dreams now lie shattered, like smashed glass on the ground,

As the world turns away, and the silence resounds.

For every child lost, a piece of hope dies,

In the heart of a mother, in the echo of cries,

We must never forget, always speak their names, and let their stories unfold,

For their futures extinguished, their lives' tales must be told.

Let us weep for the fallen, let love light the dark,

For the dreams that were stolen, we'll carry their spark,

In our hearts, they will linger, a haunting refrain,

For every little Hind, we'll bear all their pain.

AGAIN AND AGAIN

For a hundred long years, the massacres have not ceased,

The agony, the terror, and destruction have only increased.

Are you not also weary of witnessing their pain?

Again, and again, and again?

So let us make this very clear,

For every single Palestinian you kill, a thousand will rise.

For every voice you silence, you will hear a million cries.

For every time you try to empty the streets, we will fill them again.

We will bring you a million men.

Again, and again, and again.

For every time you lie with a smile, we will confront you with truth,

For every child you murder, we will give birth to our belligerent youth.

For every time you flood our screens with propaganda lies,

We will unravel them one by one,

We will open the world's eyes,

To the reality you disguise.

For every time you cry "self-defence" against a starving nation,

We will evidence your war crimes, that caused total devastation.

You have suffocated Gaza, where only death can breathe,

But we will never relent in this fight, with unwavering belief,

Until our very last breath, we shall never cease.

Today's world leaders will never stand up, or for justice preach.

Because they are probably promised a property on Trump Gaza beach!

So blinded by their hypocrisy.

By their pornography of democracy.

They are crazy and blind,

Because only the sane can see.

That one day, Palestine, Insha'Allah

Will be free!

AGAIN AND AGAIN

A Topsy-Turvy World

Bismillah.

In this topsy-turvy world, we are living in an age of big liars.

Where money is God,

And they worship their desires.

Living in an age where the rulers are the worst of the people.

Made us believe a myth that black and white were equal.

From Vietnam to Afghanistan,

And weapons of mass destruction.

The lies we have been fed, the hypocrisy and corruption.

Governments tell us that nationalism is more important than religion or truth.

But Palestine has brought the world together from the elders to the youth.

We cry "Free Free Palestine!"

But Palestine has freed us it's freed our minds.

Brainwashed, indoctrinated, we were blind.

Believing the mainstream media, hypnotised, we were in deep,

We were asleep.

A TOPSY-TURVY WORLD

Living in our dreams, not knowing the nightmare they were going through.

We didn't know what was a lie or what was true.

But we can see it clearly now, and millions over the world do too.

We march as one.

Every colour, every creed, every nationality.

Because in reality,

We know, the occupied have a right to resist the occupier.

The occupied have a right to resist the occupier,

By any means necessary, until a cease fire.

Until they get their human rights, freedom and land.

Medicines, food and water. Is that so hard to understand?

A topsy turvy world where politicians subdue us with their charms.

Speak of the horrors of the genocide, but then supply Israel with arms.

Tell us how proud they are of companies like BAE systems Elbit and Teledyne.

Complicit in the murders of thousands in Kashmir and Palestine.

In this topsy-turvy world, where the police increase violence on peaceful protestors protesting for peace!

When students come out for justice, are harassed assaulted, and beat.

NO PEACE DOVES ON THE OLIVE TREE

A topsy-turvy world, where calling for an end to genocide makes you antisemitic.

They stop at nothing to stop the truth, they truly are pathetic.

In this topsy turvy world where the evil are honoured and seen as good,

And the good are silenced or killed for their blood.

Their lives may not be our lives,

But their deaths will be our deaths for sure.

The death of our democracy, freedom of speech, of liberty and more.

Zionism is a cancer, a deadly racist disease.

Since 1897 their plans for a new world order, have year by year increased.

In 1947 they created "Is Real Hell" (Israel) ensuring it was hell, for the natives of that land.

With a continuing Nakba they murdered, stole and continued to expand.

All over the world Zionists have planned and the narrative controlled,

They have silenced, killed and imprisoned the brave, to stop their crimes being exposed.

But nothing in this world stays hidden for long.

They can lock all Gaza in a cage, but we will always sing their song.

We will be their voices when they cannot speak, until the truth is told.

A TOPSY-TURVY WORLD

We will be their voices when they cannot speak, we will never be controlled.

We will be their voices when they cannot speak, until we run out of breath.

We will be their voices when they cannot speak, until we reach our death.

And then even from our graves, our words, will be read by the brave!

NO PEACE DOVES ON THE OLIVE TREE

A TOPSY-TURVY WORLD

Back in 2016, on my first journey to Palestine, I stood by the walls of Al Aqsa masjid, by an elderly man. He was softly spoken, gentle, and kind as he offered us the sweet coffee from his flask.

He asked me to look over at the hill tops across the valley and told me that, that was where he used to live, his family's land for as long as they could remember.

Then the Zionists came and forced them out at gunpoint.

Now the white walls and gated large white houses with pools and sparkly verandas cover the hilltop. "Where do you live now?" I asked. "Oh, we didn't go far." he said.

The United Nations said they would build them temporary housing in the valley. That's where he lived, but it was never completed. It was grey breeze blocks with wires hanging and pipes across the narrow, rubble pathways. Sometimes the rubbish is thrown from the hilltop, littering the edges of this camp so only rats can survive. This poem was basically our conversation; I had to write it, although it does not do justice to the hope and the hopelessness in this voice.

A TOPSY-TURVY WORLD

Heroes

Bismillah

A Palestinian old man once told me, with tears in his eyes.
We don't need America or Saudi Arabia and their lies.
We don't need the UK; they have shown us who they are.
They change the rules and have no respect for international law.
We don't need the Arab nations; they have forgotten their Deen*.
They have forgotten their history and what Al Aqsa meant to Salahuddin!
He liberated Al Quds, promised blood shed no more,
Recognised as a hero, a humanitarian, even in times of war.
And today I see my people in Gaza, and wonder at their reality,
Standing strong amidst the bloodshed, these are the heroes of humanity.
These are the women who live like real men.
The children who have become the parent.
The brother who digs with hands in rubble, to rescue a voice.

HEROES

The mother who feeds muddy water to her child because she has no choice.

The old women who reads Quran to get starving, dying children to sleep.

A world silent at their murders because it seems their life is cheap.

The people of Gaza whose characters are explaining verses of the Quran,

Which, before now, we didn't really understand.

These are the doctors and medics who see their own families' bodies being brought in.

They have no time off work for bereavement or stress, they carry on in all the din.

In all the confusion, with no supplies.

They hear the cries, then the lies.

But they still try to save lives, try to care.

Knowing their hospitals could be bombed from the air.

We know life's not fair but this is on another level,

Because today, Gaza is dealing with the Devil.

Today, we see clearly the villains, cowards, criminals and transgressors.

The hypocrites and liars, the racists and aggressors.

The genocidal colours of Zionism shine bright.

But when will our governments wake to see the light?

We cannot wait on the courage of cowards.

NO PEACE DOVES ON THE OLIVE TREE

Our politicians have proved their pay checks overpowers.

It's time we reclaim this propaganda narrative, and rewrite.

Use our hands, our feet, our voices, pens, phones, keyboards, to fight this fight.

Pray, tweet, text, protest, email, boycott, post, march, like, speak, scream, shout or share,

just care, to change this state.

It's never too late, but there's no time to wait.

We can be the voice of those who have no voice,

no choice, no say, no pay, no fuel, no food or water.

They die from starvation, cold and disease as we sit watch the slaughter.

Watch the children are made orphans.

Watch the mother pray against her oppressor, when they drag her child away.

And what else can we say?

But these are the heroes of today.

They take away their human rights, push their backs against the wall.

Dehumanised for years but they will never see their spirits fall,

Because in their darkest hour, they reach out, hands to the sky as they kneel.

Begging to the deliverer of justice, saying 'HasbunAllah wa ni'mal-Wakil.*

HEROES

*(HasbunAllah wa ni'mal-Wakil is the prayer of prophet Abraham meaning,

Sufficient for us is Allah, and [He is] the best Disposer of our affairs.)

*Deen: Arabic word for 'religion/way of life

HEROES

Take

Bismillah

They can take their freedom,
They can take their homes,
They can take their hospitals,
They can take their bones.
They can take their human rights,
They can take their voices,
They can take their communities and take away their choices.
They can take their babies,
And call them terrorists,
They can try and wipe them out,
But they will continue to exist.
They can take away all their resources,
They can take away their land,
But one thing they will never take and never understand,
Is that, they will never be able take their courage, religion their deen*,
They will never be able to take those qualities, beliefs that can never be seen.
Never take away their dreams.
Because these people are the people of Falastine.

TAKE

But, in all this horror there is a plus.

Palestine can never be taken, because Palestine now lives in us.

So whatever Zionists of this world do,

Know for sure, we are the many, they are the few.

And as the world wakes up to all the taking, taking place,

Of tiny lives in incubators gone without a trace.

The killing of tiny babies who have never even been kissed,

And where is the outrage, the financial sanctions, or ….is there something that I've missed?

Every minute of this genocide is a shame on humanity.

How the leaders of this world stay silent is complete insanity.

Enabling this calamity.

Where is their humanity?

But we can also take.

We will take the truth and run with it.

We will show the world this Zionist shit.

We will spread the truth, spread justice and reveal all their lies!

All their propaganda, their brainwashing self-pity cries.

They may have control of the media spreading their lies,

NO PEACE DOVES ON THE OLIVE TREE

But we have the truth, and that's the biggest thorn in their side.

We will take these criminals and put them behind bars.

We will do whatever it takes to stop these bloody wars.

We will take them to the cleaners,

Show them people power cannot be controlled,

Because we have NOT,

To the Devil,

Our souls sold.

My Name

Bismillah

As I strolled along the road, for my evening walk.
I looked up at an old house, as I heard somebody talk.
A little girls face at the window sad as can be,
Gently spoke asking for help, "please will you set me free?
I was ok years ago but now my brothers and sisters have moved in.
They take my milk and biscuits, and I'm becoming really thin.
They took all my toys, so I play with stones that they threw at me, when they came.
They wanted me to bleed, to see if the colour of my blood was the same.
They sleep in my bed now with my teddy and my baby doll
And I'm squeezed in the corner sleeping up against the wall."
So, I walked closer to her house and could see her bruised little face,
dirty clothes, hair unwashed, care and protection? There was no trace.
"How did this happen?

MY NAME

Where are your parents?

They can't let this happen to you!

It's their duty to protect, ensure your safe, you're a human being too!

Shall I call the police? Maybe chid protection, I don't understand why you're so alone.

No respect, the neglect, what have done to you, you're just skin and bone."

Then to my surprise this little girl so weak and traumatised,

Began to tell a story of how her parents believed the lies.

Let's call her parents Mecc and Madi, so wealthy with oil money.

Neglected and abandoned her.

It really wasn't funny.

They stood by while her human rights were slowly stripped away.

With everything else that belonged to her, and they had nothing to say.

'I'm sure all the street must know this pain you're going through.

Does no one care? it's just not fair, why aren't they helping you?"

Then she explained it's all about land and money, and how this was planned years ago.

Her brothers and sisters wanted all that was hers,

So started taking nice and slow.

When she protested and locked her door, they just broke it down with force.

And beat her up black and blue, the violence was par for the course.

They not only stole her food and water; they took away her bike.

They chopped the olive tree that gave her shade,

They took anything they liked.

So, I listened, and I looked, and thought what can I do?

They were slowly killing her and hiding what was true.

But she was fighting,

She said 'My faith is strong; I know I will be fine.

And if you pass this way again, remember my name, it's Palestine."

She said, "please go now, as they will shoot whoever tries to help me.

My Dr was killed, and then a reporter, who tried to set me free."

I told her "No, I will shout down this street until every house is aware,

Of how they have turned away from the truth, it's disgustingly unfair."

I said "I will stand strong for you and ensure justice will be done.

MY NAME

They will pay for their crimes, and one day you too will see the sun.

I will fight for you; I will never stop until the day you're free.

You shouldn't suffer any more,

I'll always be here,

and my name?

its PSC."

NO PEACE DOVES ON THE OLIVE TREE

MY NAME

An Art form of resistance.

Following the Nakba in 1948, when 700,000 Palestinians were displaced, Tatreez (traditional Palestinian cross-stitch embroidery) became a powerful symbol of resistance.

Women continued to wear their thobes (long dresses) embroidered with Tatreez as a statement of the existence and heritage of villages lost or occupied by Israeli settlers.

Tatreez became a symbol of resistance and cultural preservation, history and heritage, showing symbols of olive branches, mountains, flowers, signs of a village lost or personal stories.

It is a deeply rooted art form, with intricate designs and patterns that have been passed down from mother to daughter for many hundreds of years. It tells stories, with each stitch, design, and motif carrying a unique meaning and narrative.

Palestinian women in occupied territories, and around the world, continue to wear embroidered clothes, thobes, bags etc as a tangible link to their heritage and identity.

In 2021, UNESCO recognised Tatreez, including its practices, skills, knowledge and rituals as part of the Intangible Cultural Heritage of Humanity, acknowledging its vital role in Palestinian arts and culture.

MY NAME

Tatreez

If you don't know me,
I am the woven threads of Palestine.
The cross.
Like 'x' marks the spot or signifies a kiss,
I am woven with much more than this,
I am woven with much more than love,
I am a blessing from above.
Rich in centuries of tradition and history,
Reflections of love and hardship in every stitch a story.
Counted threads.
And I count!
Like you'd never believe.
So much significance in my weave.
I am the crosses on the fabrics of life.
Freedom woven into threads,
My humanitarian justice overspreads.
I am resilience, liberation, emancipation.
And you will NEVER cross me out.
Because I will fight with a needle between my fingers.
Every stab of my needle is a thorn in your side.
And we stitch with pride.
Every pull of my thread is on the heart strings of humanity.

TATREEZ

Every knot manifests your sickening brutality.

A stitched, sacred cross, maybe?

Woven through our history.

Woven through our land,

Through our soil, through our sand.

Through our elders and our young,

But our talents were left unsung.

My crosses, cross cultures, cross nations, for generations across time.

I am Palestine.

Crosses, over your racism.

Your apartheid.

Crosses over your colonialism.

Over your ethnic cleansing. Your ethnocide.

We stitch with pride.

Our characters are in cross stitch beautified.

For centuries,

After,

We have died.

NO PEACE DOVES ON THE OLIVE TREE

Children of Gaza

Bismillah

These are the children of Gaza.
Taken before they were kissed.
Murdered before you were missed.
Suffocated in incubators,
Shot in the heart.
Slaughtered from the start.
Death by starvation, don't have a drop of milk to drink.
Please just take a second and think.
Not a drop of milk to drink.
These are children of Gaza.
Who once saw birds in the sky,
But all the birds have flown by,
To find somewhere to cry.
These are children of Gaza. Just like our own.
They laugh and need kisses and cry when alone.
These are children of Gaza. Just like yours and mine.
They deserve to shine, deserve to be free, with all their family.
These are children of Gaza. Like our children here.
Just want to live a peaceful life, not a life in fear.
These are children of Gaza. Like those anywhere,

CHILDREN OF GAZA

Safe in her mother's arms, they just need love and care.

These are children of Gaza. Not terrorist like they say.

They are just like our kids; all they want to do is play.

These are children of Gaza, they're our children too.

Would you not scream for justice? If this was happening to you.

These are the orphans of Gaza, without a mother or father.

As brave as can be,

We could never be like them,

Braver than a million men,

With no one to hug at night,

No one to hold them tight.

No one to comfort when bombs drop,

Or when the gunshots never stop.

These are children of Gaza.

They don't want to die.

Like the kite flying high,

They just want to be free.

Just like you and me.

Why can't they just let them be?

Why can't the leaders of this world see?

They have no military!

NO PEACE DOVES ON THE OLIVE TREE

They don't have water or food, not even a grain of rice.
I don't know who sold Palestine,
But by God,
I know who's paying the price.

CHILDREN OF GAZA

Racism Rally

Bismillah

So, when asked to write a poem I thought,
What message could I share?
What can I say about recent events?
There's racism everywhere.
But we won't despair.
Even though we know it's not fair.
It's in the press, courts, media and schools,
They try to hide it but we won't be fooled.
When people judge others by the colour of their skin,
They don't see the love or the compassion within.
They shoot daggers in my melanin.
And exactly when did skin colour become a crime?
And when did that crime become fine?
It's not the colour of your skin but what lies within.
So, do racists think their lack of colour makes them superior to him?
Did they choose the skin they're in?
Does their lack of colour make them great?
Give them pride and make them hate?
A hate from pure racism seen strong in their eyes!
Gone are KKK white hoods and long robes, now it's a jacket shirt and ties.

RACISM RALLY

But the message is the same.

They lynch and hang them with politics now, and play a dangerous game.

Then I think to myself, it makes no sense,

We've learnt nothing since the murder of Stephen Lawrence!

And what happened to Black Lives Matter?

Because they still do matter!

When he said "I can't breathe." It took my breath away!

How they all stood around with nothing to say.

It's not a few bad apples, it's from the branches to the roots,

If a plant is deprived sunlight, it can never bear fruits.

We need justice for George Floyd,

Shukri Abdi, Shireen Abu Akleh and thousands more, far and wide.

Never given a chance to tell their side.

I feel like I need to stand up and shout, "What the hell is this all about?"

The EDL have no honour, but say they carry it in their flag.

Then they burn down our streets and about nationality brag.

In his white superiority, Tommy,

Won't say his second name, don't want to give him any fame,

NO PEACE DOVES ON THE OLIVE TREE

And please excuse my language, but he's a little shit!

Paid and funded by the Zionists.

Well, it's easy to hate with friends in high places.

Because money buys faces.

And what colour are the filthy words you write on your white pages?

Black!

Think about that!

But he's not feeling well, because racism is a disease, transferred from parent to seed.

He poisons people with lies, creating division and differentiates,

With those who are different, discriminates,

But it's not their fate to hate.

So the likes of him, will never win.

Because the truth and education will set minds free.

So let us all be teachers of integrity.

Let's teach our kids to see the beauty in all shades and colours,

Be firm, show concern, like Martin Luther king said,

"Injustice anywhere, is a threat to justice everywhere."

I'll say that again.

"Injustice anywhere, is a threat to justice everywhere."

True words indeed.

RACISM RALLY

If we want our country to succeed.

We need justice in places like Palestine.

So, their children can play and be free, like yours and mine.

So please remember this,

I was born and live here too,

I love my country just like you.

NO PEACE DOVES ON THE OLIVE TREE

RACISM RALLY

What Did You Do?

Bismillah

Babies are dying, where is the humanity?
And when God asks what you did, will you plead insanity?
These are our babies, our toddlers, our kids and our teens,
Caught in a crossfire in catastrophic scenes.
Drowning in the sorrow of shattered dreams.
Innocence lost in a world shockingly unkind.
Ignoring cries for compassion, they act like they are blind.
The laughter of children is now silenced by fear,
But the supporters of genocide, their names are now clear.
Did you boycott those brands who aid genocide?
Did you shout free Palestine?
Did you scream when they cried?
So, did you stop buying L'Oréal, Nestle and Coke?
Because every penny is a bullet, it's really no joke.
Did you vote for politicians with blood on their hands?
It's that kind of thinking I can't understand.
Did you divest from Barclays, did you download the NO Thanks app?

WHAT DID YOU DO?

Because their freedom will come, and there will be a new map.

Individual actions combined, lead to significant shifts.

Support them however you can with your God given gifts.

Baby girls shot in cars and the world turns a blind eye,

If she was your daughter, would you not ask why?

Would you not cry?

Would you not try?

I'm sure you would do,

If this genocide was happening to you.

We March

Bismillah

We march with hearts that beat, never shy for justice and peace.
Our fight to free Palestine will never cease.
So let us walk where injustice dares not stand.
We will make our voices heard. We protest hand in hand.
Hearts bleed, but all agreed. Nothing in life is guaranteed.
But our protests and boycotts will succeed.
And Palestine will be freed.
This is a fight for the right to resist, for them to exist.
For humanity we never lose hope.
Never quit the fight.
Never forget Palestine.
Red green black and white.

WE MARCH

We Watched

Bismillah

While we were hanging out in our superficial worlds,
They took away your name.
No mention on Google maps.
Erased stories that bind you to this land,
Then filled in all the gaps.
And we have watched you Palestine through the day and through the night.
We watched you defend your country without an army to fight.
Trying to do what's right.
We watched your courage, your defiance, protecting what was yours.
Such peaceful resistance and resilience in your cause.
And we have been watching.
On every screen we see, every scream, every plea, but not often on the BBC.
We bring London to stand still,
And other major cities too.
Not that you ever knew.
Because they tried to hide it from world.
Tried to implement a media ban,

WE WATCHED

Doing anything, they can,

But the truth has a way of breaking through, like a whisper breaking into a roar.

Once the city streets marched to your name, they could no longer ignore.

Ignore your mothers cry at the loss of their kids.

Your courageous paramedics.

And your doctors are the bravest

Working while being shot.

They literally gave it everything they got.

Fathers holding their headless babies' bodies high for the world to see.

Did you see?

Always see.

Always be,

Of those who care.

Can you even imagine their despair?

Don't ever think that this is fair.

And we have watched those who destroyed them talk with arrogance and glee,

Their satisfaction guaranteed.

And a total absence of compassion.

Humanity not the fashion.

Then they say, "We are Gods chosen people."

What? Only the devil has chosen you!

You know that's absolutely true.

NO PEACE DOVES ON THE OLIVE TREE

Only the devil gets satisfaction,
from death and destruction.
Don't you dare blame this on God.
Don't you dare.
Don't you dare, even compare.
Your Zionist beliefs come straight from hell.
And you know that full well.
So, we marched, we spoke up,
We chanted, we boycotted, we pleaded, we cried.
Anything to stop genocide.
We tried.
But children still died.
And politicians still lied.
But every time we felt what for?
Or unsure.
Or are we actually making a difference,
are governments even listening?
We looked at you!
And we knew.
Despite the spilling of all this blood,
That you will survive, you will be fine.
Because real courage and honour is made in Palestine.

WE WATCHED

Can You?

Bismillah

Shush guys, can you hear their cries?
Can you hear the bombs, exploding from the skies?
Can you hear the tears falling from their eyes?
Can you hear their bodies, shake traumatised?
Can you hear the steps of the world, walking by?
Can you hear, the Palestinian people screaming why?
I can, and I can't, take any more of this genocide.
Sick of listening to the lies.
Sick of Starmer and his guys,
Selling Benjamin his guns.
To shoot mothers and their sons.
These are war criminals, making billions from selling arms,
With no concern to who it harms,
Who it kills,
What it destroys.
Little girls, little boys.
They just don't give a toss,
To the horror, to the loss.
Then Zippi tells Piers how poor Israel fears.
How the babies are human shields,

CAN YOU?

It's ok to blow them to bits.
She talks a load of shit!
And Zionist, little Gal asking the mirror on the wall,
Who the biggest baby killer of them all?
Israel killed more babies this year, than any accident or disease.
Now can you tell me please?
Why the hell in 2025, is no leader hearing their cries?
They feed their mouths but silence their voice.
Tell the world they got no choice.
Tell the world there's nothing to see.
Concentrate on your own liberty.
They're Hypocrites and liars.
Criminals and inhumane.
Sadistical, tyrannical,
They tell the victims, you're to blame.
Could you imagine if this was true?
That they were killing me or you?
What the hell would we do?
What the hell would we do?

Don't You Ever Think That We Have Forgotten You.

Bismillah

Don't you ever think that we have forgotten you.
We know your burden and it's ours too.
We will raise your flag,
We will hold it high, like the antlers of the stag.
On the top of the open moorland.
Proud, powerful, with eyes that landscape scan.
The breeze may ruffle its fur,
But its stands powerful undeterred.

Don't you ever think that we have forgotten you.
We know your burden and it's ours too.
We will wear your scarf
Like it's the surgical collar needed to heal after injury
Protective comforting symbolic, security

Don't you ever think that we have forgotten you.
We know your burden and it's ours too.
We admire your resilience,
your strength, perseverance.
Our luxuries have weakened our souls but we pray.
For the brave heart of a Palestinian each day.

DON'T EVER THINK THAT WE HAVE FORGOTTEN.

You have opened the eyes of the world to the hypocrites and liars.

The shocking injustice has in our hearts started fires.

No gentle breeze fanning these flames.

This genocide breeds hurricanes.

The tide has turned, and moon lost its pull.

I see silver linings on clouds darkened and dull.

The light from the truth now flickering daring to be.

Your resistance ensures Palestine will be free.

Their apartheid wall will fall.

Their lies, reveal the truth.

They play with fire, a dangerous game,

But sooner or later they'll burn in the flame.

Let's pray the world has seen the worst.

Once and for all, we can rid it of this Zionist curse.

I will. I wish

Bismillah

For every Israeli soldier, sniper, who points his gun and shoots another child.

I can't stay calm, anymore, I scream and cry, I go crazy, I go wild.

If only I could get my hands on you.

Do you know what I would do?

I WILL. I WISH

Chant For Our March

Bismillah

Starmer, Starmer you can't hide,
We charge you with genocide.
It's on your watch that thousands died.
We charge you with genocide.
You do nothing while your nation cried.
We charge you with genocide.
People see your hypocrisy far and wide.
We charge you with genocide.
All we hear are lies, lies, lies.
We charge you with genocide.
Israel's war crimes can no longer be denied,
We charge you with genocide.
You blindly support Israel, with the devil allied,
We charge you with genocide.
Israeli war crimes you brush aside ...so
We charge you with genocide!
Hold Israel to account? You've not even tried.
We charge you with genocide.
Ignore crimes against humanity and smile with pride.
We charge you with genocide.
For your support and funding of this apartheid.
We charge you with genocide.

CHANT FOR OUR MARCH

Palestinians fight for freedom is justified.
We charge you with genocide.
Their resistance is heroic and seen worldwide.
We charge you with genocide.
You need a kick, up your backside!
We charge you with genocide.
Starmer, Starmer you can't hide.
We charge you with genocide.
And we charge all those who are silent, as complicit in this genocide.
From multi-conglomerate giants to individuals near,
You know who you are, and the end is near.
History will stand as our judge in this fight.
Establishing the wrongs and our quest for what is right.
So, one day you will see,
From the river to the sea.
Palestine will be free
Insha'Allah.

NO PEACE DOVES ON THE OLIVE TREE

Printed in Dunstable, United Kingdom